IDENTIFYING YOUR
DREAM JOB

And Telling Your Story to Get It

By

Kim Brushaber

About The Author

Kim Brushaber first started working in a hiring capacity as a volunteer campus recruiter for her first job out of college. It was her responsibility to meet with potential college candidates and gather their resumes to include in a large resume book. She helped to determine which candidates should advance through the process.

She then worked for seven and a half years for a company that built Applicant Tracking Software. Applicant Tracking Software was first used to help automate the hiring process by tracking a candidate from the time they submitted their resume electronically until they signed an offer.

In 2008, Kim went to work for a recruiting firm. She helped to identify quality candidates for companies during a huge economic downturn.

In 2009, Kim started her own company, Bridge ATX where she worked with job seekers to help them find jobs during the economic downturn. She held several "Get Hired" seminars where she gathered career coaches from across Austin to come together to work with candidates to help them with all of their job search questions. She realized that the regular resources for the job search process were not helping job seekers when the market was flooded. She started "Connection Conversations" to help assist candidates with topics that were not normally covered in the variety of job seeker groups across Austin.

In 2010, Kim partnered with Austin Career Coaching to help to better equip candidates with networking skills. During this time she learned a lot from veteran career coaches while also using her knowledge to try the job search process from a different angle. She launched an executive networking job clublet that was specifically for the problems encountered by executive job seekers. She split her time between career coaching and helping companies to improve their hiring processes.

In 2011, Kim went back to work for a recruiting firm. She continues to work with job seekers in both a career coaching capacity and a headhunting capacity. Her favorite part of her week is the hour that she gets to spend with the executive job seeker group.

Nothing thrills her more than to watch someone who has been struggling through their job search fine their AHA moment when their job search becomes clearer. Hope is a powerful thing.

Acknowledgements

Although it is impossible to acknowledge every single person I have encountered as a job seeker or a hiring manager, I would like to take a moment to thank a few specific people without whom this journey would not have been possible.

Austin Career Coaches – Donna Fox, Stan Tyler and Pauline Hoehn

Copy Editors – Peggy Richmond and Melanie Wise

Workbook Reviewers – Greg Effrein, Larry Wallace, Jan Hames, Bill Herring, Barbara Clauson, Cary Peele, Michael Jordan, Paul Viebrock, Rick Landwehr and Venky Vadlamani

Another special thanks to Mark Thames, without whom I would not have been finally sparked to post this workbook online for all to use.

To all the Job Seekers out there who I have helped through your Career Transition, I hope that you are now in a job that leaves you feeling very fulfilled. If not, I hope that you continue your search until you find it.

I also need to acknowledge my family, without whom I would not have the ambition to do this.

About This Workbook

Many people have reported that the first review of this workbook left them feeling very overwhelmed by the concepts addressed inside it. Please understand that this is normal. If Story Telling were easy, you wouldn't need this workbook in the first place.

Several sections of the workbook ask you to list twenty items. These items require a lot of thought and should not be completed in one sitting. Jot down a few ideas and come back to the list over the course of several days. This will allow you to get a deeper understanding for the concepts that will create your story. You might want to carry around a small notebook as you go about your day in case another idea comes to you when you are not actively working on the workbook.

When you are ready to start outlining your stories try to work on only a few outlines at a time. As you start to uncover more of the story, more narratives will come to mind. Make sure that you jot down quick notes for the other stories that you wish to tell.

[You might want to consider adding a bit more about how the workbook is organized (parts 1, 2, and 3) and how to use the workbook. I like the first part here, and it could be expanded]

Why Should You Tell Your Story?

This workbook is focuses on Story Telling from a Job Transition perspective. Types of Job Transitions might include:

- I want the job that I am doing now to be more rewarding
- I want to advance my career to the next level
- I want to take on a new job that is similar to something that I have done before
- I want to consider a new job that may not be similar to anything I have done before
- I want to start a new business
- I want to improve a business that I already run
- I am trying to decide whether I want to continue working or retire (or maybe come out of retirement)
- I am reentering the workforce after being gone for a while

However, Story Telling is important no matter where you are in your life. The act of defining your story allows you to gain better power and perspective on the things that you have accomplished in your life. There's never a better time to be proud of yourself than today.

Story Telling does not end. Your story continues with you. It's a great idea to work on your story even when you are not looking to make a transition.

A Note on Bragging

I did a Google Search for "Why is it so hard for people to brag about themselves?" The first few answers today came back with something along the lines of "Why people who brag about themselves are so annoying".

That result caused me to wonder, at what point in our society do we suddenly get shamed for being a "braggart"? How do you arrive at a darker place where you can't tell other people what you are good at? When did we start to feel guilty for telling ourselves that we're good at something? We start to become ashamed when people pay us a compliment. Sadly, some of us will go so far as to argue heavily with our admirer, attempting to convince them their esteem is unwarranted. That's just crazy.

Unfortunately for job seekers, the entire job search process is all about telling people what you're really truly good at. We have to learn how to brag about ourselves again.

Everyone has natural talents with which they were born. If you look deep enough, you'll find that there are some things you are better at than anyone else you know. This workbook will teach you how to identify your natural talents and then how to confidently tell someone else all about them.

This process of discovering and renewing your bragging rights will be easier for some than others. For instance, some people have been unexpectedly forced to make a job or career transition, while others face the challenge of underemployment. These and other situations contribute to a defeated or deflated perspective and frequently lead people to question whether or not they were EVER good at anything they used to think they'd mastered. However, realize that every single person out there is challenged to be their own best advertisement in some way. The fact that you're reading this workbook means that you've taken the first step towards admitting it. And, that's the first step to making a change.

Part One: Drawing the Lines

Within your job transition or job search lies the perfect opportunity to redefine yourself. At the end of the day and after much exploration, you may still decide to go back to doing what you have always done. But at that point, you'll go back because you've discovered that's where you truly belong, not that you have no other options.

So, the very first part of your job search is outlining the places where you want to play. There are millions of jobs out there. How do you figure out which one *you* want?

The first guidelines to identify for you are:

- What do you love to do?
- What are you really good at?
- What are the boundaries that would keep you from accepting a job offer?

After that, you can start to color in between the lines, deciding what kind of environment you'd want to operate in and what your ideal reward system looks like.

This is the basis and foundation against which you will compare every single job offer/opportunity.

Let me illustrate how this works for me. On highly stressful days, I tell people "I'm two bad days away from selling everything I own and moving to Bora Bora". Now, you never know, one day I might even make good on the threat. Some people who know me think I haven't done so yet because it's a risky adventure. Nothing could be further from the truth. I'm a risky adventurer every day. The reality is that I haven't yet done it for several reasons:

1) I've never been to Bora Bora, so I'm not sure if I'd really like it. *Translation – I don't know if I would love it there more than here.*
2) If I went there without a plan, I would be bored after sitting on the beach doing nothing but drinking margaritas for two weeks straight. *Translation – I know that I would get bored quickly and I don't know how to apply my strengths to a foreign location.*
3) I have no idea what it would cost me to live in Bora Bora. *Translation – I don't know where to set my boundaries so that I could live there comfortably.*

So, while your current dream may not be to take off and move to Bora Bora, you do have to be able to define the dream.

The Math – A Reality Check

Let's do a little math:

24 hours a day x 7 days a week = 168 hours in a week for every single week in your life.

Let's just SAY that you get 8 hours of sleep a night (8 hours x 7 days = 56 hours). That would leave us with 112 waking hours every single week in your life.

Now let's SAY that you work only 8 hours a day, 5 days a week (8 hours x 5 days = 40 hours). That means that 35% of your waking hours are spent at work. Not bad...

But then (again being generous), let's say it takes you 30 minutes to get ready for work and that you work 30 minutes away from your house. Add in an extra 1 ½ hours to your work day. Now, let's also add in that pesky lunch hour in the middle of the day. Some of us use it for personal reasons, but most of us either skip it entirely OR we go out to work with coworkers where we continue to talk about work. That extra 2 ½ hours x 5 days brings our REALISTIC work hours per week to be (8 hours + 2 ½ hours x 5 days = 52.5 hours).

This means 47% of our waking hours are devoted to work. And, this INCLUDES weekend hours (when you're not supposed to be working).

How many of you ONLY work 40 hours a week? How many have a longer commute in traffic? How many of you can't stop talking about work even after you've left work? How many go home and continue to work there each night?

So, even if you are working the bare minimum hours at a full time job, you are still occupying 50% of your time WITH WORK.

I don't know about you, but I want to make damn sure that if I'm going to commit half of my life to something, I am going to LOVE what I do.

What do you LOVE?

It's essential to figure out what you LOVE to do when you are in a job transition. You really should accept no less of yourself.

Does that mean that because I LOVE to eat Macaroni and Cheese that I should become a taste tester for Macaroni and Cheese? Um... Probably not... As much as I love it, I would HATE it if I had to eat Macaroni and Cheese for a week straight (let alone for a living).

Instead, when you think of what you LOVE to do think of:

- What drives/motivates you?
- What brings you joy?
- What gives you energy?
- What feeds your soul?

I also want you to think along these lines – if all of your bills were paid, but you still decided that you wanted to work – what would you choose to do?

Some of us might initially say "If all my bills were paid, I would never work again." That could be because you are just worn out and exhausted from what you have been doing. Or, perhaps you just lack creativity. So, I'm going to ask you to dig deeper.

If you still say, "I would go and be a bum and backpack around Europe," Well, then in that case, I will let you add it to your list of LOVES and possible career choices. Some people do make a living from traveling around the world.

The other thing I want you to do is to momentarily step away from a Job Title or role.

For the activity below, in no particular order, consider what are the twenty things that you really LOVE to do. Then, circle the top five in the list.

To assist you a little, here are my top 5 loves:

1) I LOVE to give people A HA moments and help them to transform themselves from an unhappy state to a joyful state. I love to make a difference in people's lives for the better.
2) I get my energy from working with people. When I work at home by myself my energy decreases, but when I go and talk to people and work with them, my energy goes up.
3) I LOVE having the freedom to do different things every single day. Repetition bores me.
4) I LOVE problem solving. Give me a game/puzzle/problem and I'm so excited when I figure it out.
5) I LOVE building long lasting relationships built on truth and honesty.

Okay, so now it's your turn. Go ahead and start. Come back if you need to.

1) _____
_____
_____

2) _____
_____
_____

3) _____
_____
_____

4) _____
_____
_____

5) _____
_____
_____

6) _____
_____
_____

7) _____
_____
_____

8) _____
_____
_____

9) _____
_____
_____

10) _____
_____
_____

11) _____
_____
_____

12) _____
_____
_____

13) _____
_____
_____

14) _____
_____
_____

15) _____
_____
_____

16) _____
_____
_____

17) _____
_____
_____

18) _____
_____
_____

19) _____
_____
_____

20) _____
_____
_____

Now that you have your list, make sure that you have circled your TOP 5 items. Start to look at every job opportunity to see if it meets your list of LOVES. Ideally, your next job will include your top 5. If not, consider whether or not you can do something else in your life (volunteering, etc) where you can still incorporate that love into your life. If it is one of your TOP 5 loves, it needs to be in your life somewhere or you're not going to be reaching your full potential for happiness.

Also, take time to consider whether or not these loves can easily be grouped into categories. If it is just a repetition of the same theme, consolidate them and come up with MORE loves. If it isn't really repetition, then you know that that group of elements MUST be in your next position.

For example you might list:

1) I LOVE to travel to exotic places.
2) I LOVE to lie on the beach and soak up rays.
3) I LOVE to adventure to far off lands.

In this case, if you look at your career choices, the combination of the three takes you down a particular set of paths. For example, looking at all three together you might consider becoming a bartender in a rain forest. However, just one of those ideas could point you down that same path.

In this case I would consolidate all three into one love – your love for travel, adventure and white sandy beaches. ☺

On the other hand, you might also have 3 items that SOUND the same but may lead you to very different paths.

1) I LOVE to help people who are in unfortunate situations.
2) I get a lot of energy from talking about things that affect the environment.
3) I LOVE to work in my garden.

Love #1 might lead you to being a social worker. Love #2 might lead you to working on a job dealing with renewable energy. Love #3 might lead you to working in a nursery.

In this case, while they all point in a humanitarian direction, you should keep them separate because they could lead you in radically different directions.

I had a job seeker tell me that he was having problems trying to determine what he LOVES because his loves have nothing to do with his profession. He told me that he LOVES his kids. So, I started to ask him what he loved about his interaction with his children. Like any proud papa, he told me that he has loved watching them grow up into what they have become today. I pointed out that perhaps he might also love a job where he was able to take an idea at its infancy and drive it all the way through to a grand result. Of course there are lots of other reasons for him to love his children, but through the course of our conversation, he discovered something else about an aspect of a job that he would love.

So, I challenge you to really dig deep and find out what gets you excited. Think of the happiest moments of your life to uncover your loves. Then consider whether or not you could apply that love from that moment and convert it to something that you might be able to do within your career.

Remember that if you can't find ways for your job to allow you to do things that you love, be sure to add it in somewhere in your life.

What are you GOOD at?

Knowing what you're GOOD at is essential when finding a job. The question will come up in a variety of different ways. I'll outline some of them further down in the workbook. Some things you are good at will align with the things you LOVE and some of them will not. All of them will help you to promote yourself going forward.

The first thing I want you to do is ask yourself what you think you are really good at. Think back to times when people have complimented you on your efforts/results. Think back on some of your proudest moments, both work related and non-work related. Is there anything that you can think of that you really are better at than anyone else?

Now, identifying your strengths is not something that can easily be done all by yourself. For this one, unless you've already done a whole lot of self analysis, you will want to get help from other people.

After you've created your own starting list of things you're GOOD at, identify 5 – 10 people who know you very well. Talk to past employers, co-workers, subordinates, and don't forget friends and people that you work with in a volunteer capacity. Ask them for a few minutes of their time to share their observations of where you excel. You can do this over the phone, face to face, via email, via an online survey tool or take the information from your LinkedIn referrals. It really doesn't matter as long as you get the information.

Ask them:

1) When you talk about me, what do you tell people that I do?
2) What do you think that I'm really good at?
3) In what ways have I helped you?
4) What do you think I should be the most proud of?
5) What do I do better than anyone you know? Or, in what ways am I unique?
6) What other good qualities do you think I have?

From this point, you should start to get a pretty clear idea of where your strengths lie. If not, then reach out to more people and ask them the same questions to see if you get different responses.

My favorite part of this exercise is that you get an opportunity to find out what your friends really think about you. Frequently, you'll end up very surprised. We don't typically realize how much people really honor and respect what we do.

You might also find that the responses you are getting from others are different from the ones you have generated for yourself. If that is the case for you, you have two options:

- You can educate people about strengths you have of which they were unaware.
- You can reevaluate your strengths and begin to highlight what you naturally do best rather than what you have always thought you did best.

If you are naturally good at something, you normally will not view that item as a strength. We tend to think that if it's easy for us to do it, it's easy for the rest of the world, too. This will cause many of us to overlook some of our greatest strengths. So, getting other people involved will help you to identify areas where you have natural abilities that you would ordinarily overlook.

Now I want you to list your top 20 strengths and circle the favorite TOP 5 strengths that you have.

1) _____
   _____
   _____

2) _____
   _____
   _____

3) _____
   _____
   _____

4) _____
   _____
   _____

5) _____
   _____
   _____

6) _____
   _____
   _____

7) _____
   _____
   _____

8) _____
   _____
   _____

9) _____
   _____
   _____

10) _____

_____

_____

11) _____

_____

_____

12) _____

_____

_____

13) _____

_____

_____

14) _____

_____

_____

15) _____

_____

_____

16) _____

_____

_____

17) _____

_____

_____

18) _____

_____

_____

19) _____

_____

_____

20) _____

_____

_____

What are your BOUNDARIES?

This question is important because it allows you to identify limits.

You may find that you REALLY love to play video games. You may find that you are REALLY good at playing video games. However, lots of people also love video games and are willing to work really cheaply and sacrifice things in order to get paid to do that all day every day. If you need to make six figures a year, you won't be able to walk into an entry level position at a gaming studio and demand that tomorrow. But, if you don't have a particular budget to hold you back, then there's NOTHING standing in the way of walking into that gaming studio and asking what you can do to help TODAY.

Boundaries can come from a lot of different places. I'll help to get you to think down this path by throwing a few questions to you. Just remember though, everyone's boundaries are different and personal, so don't let my questions stop you from identifying your true boundaries.

I also want you to consider which boundaries that you identify are real and which are not real. Frequently, I talk to people who are coming straight out of school and they want to be making six figures within the next two years and they want to own their own company. While highly ambitious and achievable by the few super humans in our midst (or if you have parents with tons of money), this outcome is one that most of us are not equipped to pull off. Therefore, I would consider this a boundary that is not real. Instead, I encourage each person to look at what is realistic. How can the next job teach them how to run their own business, keeping in mind the goal of owning their own business within two years?

I also want you to identify what are your "Nice to Haves" and "Deal Breakers." "Nice to Haves" help you highlight what your top goal(s) would be if you could have everything you want (and of course we should all have everything we want). "Nice to Haves" are things that we could do without, but they should be considered in your decision. "Deal Breakers" tell you if you see this condition exists/does not exist then you MUST walk away from the deal no matter how good it is in any other aspect.

Understand that boundaries can also change over time. When going through this workbook at this moment, project your boundaries within the coming six months. Feel free to come back to this workbook at any point in the future to reevaluate.

First, I'll pose questions to get you started thinking about standard boundaries. For each question, respond as you would upon accepting a position within the next six months. Weight how strongly you feel about each of these boundaries. Using a scale of 1 to 5, rank each answer, using 1 to indicate that you feel this boundary is not as important to you. Use a 5 to indicate that this boundary is an absolute deal breaker, and non-negotiable.

If you have other people who depend upon you, consider which of your boundaries are YOUR boundaries and which of your boundaries are based on the needs/expectations of the people who depend on you.

1) Do you have a boundary regarding relocating to another city (in the state, country or world)?

2) Do you have a boundary regarding the amount that you would be willing to travel?

3) Do you have a boundary regarding the minimum amount of money you must make in order to support your budget?

4) Do you have a boundary regarding an income goal that you have set for yourself (either by yourself or with someone else)?

5) Do you have a boundary regarding the number of hours you are willing to work in a week?

6) Do you have a boundary regarding lifestyle choices (*e.g.*, going to the gym every day)?

7) Do you have a boundary regarding benefit plans?

8) Do you have a boundary regarding stability and job security?

9) Do you have any physical boundaries (*e.g.*, can't stand for 8 hours a day)?

10) Do you have any other commitments that provide boundaries (*e.g.*, need to pick up my child from school every day at 3 PM)?

In order to help you consider other boundaries that you have, look back over some of your loves. Pick one of your loves that you are not doing in your career now.   Why aren't you doing it? Frequently this will uncover additional boundaries for you. Take the time to consider whether or not these are real boundaries.

I had a job seeker who said he loves to cook. So I asked him why he didn't want to be a chef. He told me that when he was younger he used to work at a restaurant.   While he loved to create new recipes to great reviews, he found that there were a lot of elements of that job he didn't like at all. He didn't like the crazy hours that he had to work. He didn't like the repetition of cooking the items the same way every single time. He didn't like to retrain the staff because of all the turnover in the restaurant industry.   As he continued to go down his list of why he doesn't want to be a chef anymore, he never realized that he was spilling out his long list of items that were his boundaries. All of them could be translated back to helping him define what kind of a work environment he wanted to be in and what kind of a work environment would never work from him.

We will get into more boundaries surrounding the type of reward system that you need and the type of culture within which you desire to work later in the workbook. For now, think only about what are your TOP 5 deal breakers. What are the five most important boundaries (not included in the questions above) that you need to consider (they might be deal breakers or they might be strong "nice to haves").

My Top Five Deal Breaker Boundaries Are:

1) _____
   _____
   _____

2) _____
   _____
   _____

3) _____
   _____
   _____

4) _____
_____
_____

5) _____
_____
_____

The Next Five Most Important Boundaries to me are:

1) _____
_____
_____

2) _____
_____
_____

3) _____
_____
_____

4) _____
_____
_____

5) _____
_____
_____

What Are Your IDEAL Reward Systems?

Every organization has different ways of rewarding its employees. I've separated this discussion from the boundary section because I think that we are all somewhat flexible in regards to the way we are rewarded. However, if we are truly looking to get into the job that we will LOVE then we need to consider what our IDEAL REWARD SYSTEMS are.

Everyone appreciates different rewards for their work. So, take this time to consider what best motivates you.

Evaluate these statements and rank them accordingly from the most important (1) to the least important (9):

I prefer to be rewarded by:
_____ Bonuses and other forms of increased compensation
_____ Recognition within my team
_____ Recognition within my company
_____ Recognition granted by top level executives
_____ Company stock options that will lead to bigger future payoffs
_____ Having more flexible work hours
_____ Being granted greater authority over decisions
_____ Luxuries that I would not normally treat myself to
_____ Means that are not mentioned here

Based on your unique preferences toward rewards for a job well done, you will be able to better communicate with someone who is hiring you what kind of rewards you would most like to receive.

After going through that exercise, you have probably thought of additional ways where you might like to be rewarded for your work.

Please use this space to indicate any other ways that you'd like to be rewarded:

_____

_____

_____

What Is Your IDEAL Culture?

Culture is another area that might help you to define some boundaries. I find, however, that frequently people are willing to compromise on some culturally related items.

Corporate or organizational culture is difficult to assess before you're actually working within a company. You might hear, "They have a great culture," but what the person conveying that perception really means could vary from the company offers some fun perks to all the employees work together and get along well to everyone must believe, behave, and look the same way (and I personally like that type of conformity).

So, take a moment to consider what is important to you in a company's cultural makeup. As we did with boundaries, I'll pose some standard cultural questions for you to consider. For your answer, think about your preference for the first situation posed within the question versus your preference for the second situation posed within the question. Use the score box to indicate which side you prefer. Indicate the strength of your preference using one to three Xs where (X) indicates that you mildly prefer that choice and (XXX) indicates that you strongly prefer that choice.

Do you prefer an environment where:

Score	Option 1	Score	Option 2
	You have a lot of management's attention/input		You are generally left alone to do your own work at your own pace
	You work your way up the ladder based on the time that you devote to the company		The best person for the job moves up the ladder the quickest
	Each day is predictable and repeatable		Everything changes on you every single day
	Processes are defined and things flow from one side to another		Processes are loosely defined and you are streamlining chaos that comes in from all different directions
	People just do their work and go home		Teammates spend a lot of time together after work hours
	People keep to themselves during the day		People are constantly walking around the office collaborating together
	Hierarchies in an organization are respected		Employees at every level have access to the CEO
	Honesty is appreciated in measured amounts		Open feedback is appreciated and acted on swiftly
	Your role is the same for the duration of time in a position		You job position could change on you quarterly
	The company clearly lays out the growth plan for your position		You're given your own ability to lay out your personal growth plan within the company
	You have the same roles and responsibilities for a number of years		You are working on the cutting edge of technology where roles and responsibilities are always changing
	The company is structured and orderly		The company has a very loose structure
	There is a training process		Everything is trial by fire and you are expected to learn as you go
	You are evaluated by your boss		You are evaluated by your peers

Another part of company culture involves perks that you might receive at a company. Most of them are nice to haves, but there might be some that you particularly like.

Consider some of these perks:

- Free Vending Machines
- Free Meals
- Gourmet Coffee and Cappuccino Machines
- Free Adult Beverages
- Recreational Activities (Ping Pong, Basketball, *etc.*)
- Work Out Facility on Location
- Day Care Facility on Location
- Working From Home
- Flexible Work Hours
- Time Sharing
- Fully Paid Medical Coverage
- Dental Coverage or Eye Care Coverage
- Extended Vacation Benefits
- Concierge Service
- Company Sponsored Events/Happy Hours
- Employee Contests
- Ergonomic Workstations

Think about the different companies that you have worked for in the past. What was their culture like? What did you like about it? What didn't you like about it?

If you have aspects of culture that are extremely important to you – start asking people at your target companies (either current employees or previous employees) if those aspects of corporate culture are present at that company.

Use the space below to list any additional aspects of culture that are important to you.

_____

_____

_____

_____

_____

_____

_____

_____

Reviewing the Lines

At this point, a picture should be starting to become clear to you. You should now be able to clearly identify what you LOVE to do and how that might translate to a job that you will LOVE to go to every day. You should now be able to clearly identify your TOP 5 Strengths that you can use to communicate to a company when convincing them to hire you for a position. You should now understand what your Deal Breaker and Nice to Have Boundaries are that you can review when deciding what kinds of positions you would like to take and which ones will not work for you. You should now understand how you like to be rewarded so that you can communicate that to a future employer in order for them to help motivate you to do a better job. You should now understand the types of culture that you would like to work in.   All of these aspects are important to help you to define what you future role and company will look like.

Now that you know what YOU WANT in order to find an ideal position, we'll shift our focus to helping you to start to tell people what you want and why they should hire you to take on that role within that company.

Part Two: Onto the STORY TELLING

By now you should be starting to get an idea of what lines can be drawn when you are defining the type of future role into which you'd like to step. That's part one of the job hunting equation. Once you know what you are looking for, it's on to step two — finding someone who is willing to hire you for that role. But, in order for someone to know whether they want to hire you, you must be able to tell your story in a compelling, succinct way.

Story Telling is used in a variety of ways during a job search. In this workbook, we will cover Story Telling in these situations:

1) 30 Second Introductions
2) Networking
3) Resume
4) Interview

Clarity, Focus and Simplicity

First and foremost, a good story teller shares a Story Telling message that is easily understood by others. If other people don't understand your stories, they don't know how to help you with your search and they certainly don't understand how you might fit into a future position at their organization or elsewhere.

Review your TOP 5 strengths. If you explained your TOP 5 strengths to a fifth grader, would they understand what you were talking about? As adult professionals, we too often revert to work mode," speaking in jargon or industry colloquialisms. To the uninitiated or layperson, your strengths may seem highly technical and difficult to understand.

Let me give you a personal example to illustrate this point. During the late 1990s, I worked in a technical support role. I certainly couldn't explain to most people the intricacies of what I did every single day. I never had the same day twice. However, I managed to come up with an explanation that even a kindergartner could understand. When people asked me what I did I said:

> "I work with people to put band-aids on their problems until the development team can create a more permanent solution."

Think about that expression. Can you clearly understand what my job was? Can you see the value that I added for the organization as well as the customer?

I talk to people constantly who tell me that they design some sort of technical jargon piece of integrated circuit board machinery that is used in things that I can't ever dream of understanding. I desperately want to understand what they do, but I feel like they are speaking to me in a foreign language where I'm only able to pick up a very few words. By the time I think I've processed the words they've given me, they are eight more sentences into the conversation and I'm completely lost.

So, stop now and translate your TOP 5 strengths into something a child can understand. When you're done, grab your kid and read it to them to see if they get what you do. If you don't have children, borrow a friend's child. Just call them up on the phone and ask to speak to their kid for a minute. If you don't have friends who have children, stop a random person (not a child — that would be creepy) at a random place like a grocery store, try out your new description, and see if they understand what you just said to them.

Here's space to write down your TOP 5 Strengths:

1) _____
   _____
   _____

2) _____
   _____
   _____

3) _____
   _____
   _____

4) _____
   _____
   _____

5) _____
   _____
   _____

It's okay if your descriptions aren't perfect yet. You will improve them as you go along. Just get started moving your head in this direction.

Go back and review some of your statements (loves, strengths, boundaries, *etc.*) that you have made in the workbook up until now. How clear are your statements? Would they make sense to other people? Are they complete sentences? If someone were to pick up and read any of your sentences with no background information, would they understand what it means? Or, would you need another five minutes to explain your idea/concept?

As we continue through the workbook, I want you to strive for clarity in all your thoughts and expressions. The clearer you can be to yourself, the easier it will be for a prospective employer to understand you.

Story, Action and Result

In the remainder of the workbook, we will focus on Story, Action, and Result. This framework is an essential tool as we work through the remaining exercises.

I've provided the basic Story, Action, Result template below and have included several additional templates for use in the Workbook Appendix. Using these templates, illustrate each of your TOP 5 Strengths within three different stories, highlighting how you exhibited your strengths in each situation. Of course, the more stories you can document, the more practice you will have "bragging on yourself" and the more likely you are to appear as a stronger employment candidate.

Pick one of your TOP 5 strengths for this exercise.

STORY

You should be able to tell your story in a minute and a half or less. During a networking conversation, you only have about two minutes before the person you are conversing with becomes distracted from what you are saying. In an interview environment, you shouldn't spend more than two minutes answering any question in order to allow time for more questions or further clarification.

The best way to abbreviate a story is to tell it over and over and over again. Also, consider exactly what it is that you want to say in your story. Sometimes the details that you share are really not essential to the story. Be careful to consider how that story specifically relates to the Strength that you identified. The same story can be used to highlight other strengths as well.

Frequently when you tell your story for the first time, you will find that there are several strengths highlighted within the story. At that point you should break your story into separate pieces so that you can showcase the strength that has been requested.

I had a job seeker who started telling me about a situation where she had inherited a very difficult client when she entered into a new role at an organization. When she told me her story I started to hear several different minor stories within the main story. One story ended up breaking into these several smaller stories pertaining to:

- *Requirements Gathering - Gathered Client Expectations*
- *Client Negotiations - Refined and Reset Client Expectations*
- *Defining Processes - Established New Policies Regarding Interacting with Clients*
- *Managing Large Projects - Prioritized Major Defects for Upcoming Release of New Product*
- *Customer Satisfaction - Increased Customer Retention by 70%*
- *Closing Deals - Acquired 20 New Customer Contracts*

Each of these smaller stories showcased different strengths.

ACTION

This is the part where you get to say WHAT YOU DID given the circumstances. See if you can come up with one sentence (maybe two) that describe your actions in the story that you have identified.

If you start to hear that you took several actions, this is a key indicator that you have more than one story that you are telling.

Sometimes when we consider our stories they take us back to a negative situation. The best way to convert a negative story into a positive one is to consider the actions that you took. It is within the actions that we can start to understand and believe, "I did this good thing in that bad situation."

RESULT

This is what people really care about. What was the result based on what you did? If possible, use very specific numbers to outline the result.

- Did the action result in a 50% return on investment?
- Did you reduce costs by 20%?
- Did you close a deal worth $250K?
- Did you increase customer retention by 15%?

People use numbers to quantify success. What are your numbers?

Frequently we don't think about our metrics until we are in the midst of a performance review. What metrics were you judged by in that role? What did you accomplish?

Sometimes with soft skills, we end up having a "fuzzy result" from our efforts. Consider the impact that your actions had on the company and who it affected.

I had a job seeker whose strength revolved around how she was able to carefully orchestrate client interactions. She had another team member who was notorious to for saying the wrong thing to the client. In meetings, she would sit across the table and watch for non-verbal queues when the client would start to become upset with this team member. When she saw the tension start to build, she would carefully interject statements that diffused the situation. She began to master this so well that people wouldn't even notice that she was doing it. While she knew what her very deliberate actions were, she wasn't sure what the results were other than that she had averted a fight.

I asked her what would have happened had she not intervened. She didn't really know. She wasn't sure that they would have lost the client because they had a very tight contract. She wasn't sure if the other team member would have lost their job. However, what we uncovered was that she saved a lot of time during the meetings by avoiding the 30 minute argument that would have likely have taken place had she not been there. Because these daily meetings were only an hour long, she could comfortably say that they were able to accomplish things in one week that would have normally taken two weeks to accomplish. Ultimately this saved them a month of development time which allowed them to complete the project on time and under budget.

POSITION HELD

This allows you to identify where you were working at the time the story took place. This will become useful if you are using a chronological resume format. It also helps when people ask for specific examples of what you did in your various positions.

When you are reviewing your stories, you may see that some positions have very few stories. This gives you the opportunity to dig deeper into what you did at that position to be able to add more stories to the mix.

BULLET POINT

This is where you take the action and result and combine it into something that can be used on your resume to indicate how you exhibit a given strength.

Story, Action, Result Example 1

STRENGTH
Networking

STORY
When I worked at a staffing company, I was required to make 100 outbound phone calls daily in order to drum up more business. I thought it was better to meet with and interact with that many people at networking events rather than just picking up the phone and calling them for metrics' sake. I started to attend a variety of networking events and quickly became known as the Networking Queen of Austin. I did such a good job picking up clients we had never worked with before that I was asked to talk to all of the Managing Directors about my ability to build stronger and better networks.

ACTION
I adapted the logic of the company vision from making 100 phone calls a day to meeting with over 100 people at networking events on a weekly basis, transforming the way that business got closed.

RESULT
In one quarter, during a period where few people were hiring, I was able to secure $250K in deals from new clients.

POSITION HELD
Business Development Manager – a Staffing Company

BULLET POINT
Transformed business processes from a call-oriented model to a network-oriented model resulting in $250K in new business in one quarter during a period of time when few companies were hiring

Story, Action, Result Template – Your Turn

STRENGTH

STORY

ACTION

RESULT

POSITION HELD

BULLET POINT

Telling Your Story at Networking Events

Networking Events are simply little bitty pieces of conversations. Within conversations, you tell stories. Telling a good story will make you memorable to people.

How often have you met someone and had a conversation with them and then you run back into them a week later and you can still remember the story that they told you at the last networking event? You might remember their child's activities. You might remember their hobbies. There are a variety of different things that people might remember about you. Finding common bonds with the other individual helps them to remember you. Use Networking Events to your advantage to help people remember what you did for a company. This helps when they run into someone later; they can share your story with potential employers.

There are three parts to a networking event conversation – introduction, conversation, and closing. My networking workbook will go into MUCH greater detail on all of these pieces. However, for the sake of Story Telling, I'm going to focus on just the first two.

Introducing Yourself

The very first thing that happens when you start a new networking conversation is an exchanged introduction. Sometimes it's simply "Hi I'm Kim, what's your name and what do you do?" However, I encourage you to take an extra step and provide a little more detail in order to entice people to have a richer conversation with you.

The best simple networking introduction is:

- Name
- Functional Area
- Company
- I AM statement
- Value statement

Your name should be pretty self explanatory. We learn how to do that when we are toddlers. ☺

Your functional area should be a broad swipe to set the conversation. If you are in a room full of people without a job related connection then you should say something as simple as "I work in Sales", "I work in Operations", "I work in Support" or whatever it is that you do. However, if you say you work in sales and you're at a sales convention, people are going to look at you and think you have lost your mind. In those cases you can be more specific about your discipline.

For your company, you should state the company that you currently work for. However, there are times when job seekers do not have a current company. In that case, I suggest you say something like "I was formerly with COMPANY NAME" or "I was previously with COMPANY NAME". It allows people to recognize that you are a job seeker without you having to say so. It also allows people to have a frame of reference as to the type of companies you have worked with most recently. It's also okay to say "I'm formerly with a small tech startup" or something like that. You don't always have to use the company name.

For your I AM statement, this is the first part where you start to tell your story. Consider all of your strengths and what you are really good at. If you could pick a phrase to summarize your favorite strength what would it be?

I encourage you NOT to use common phrases like "I'm a people person" because lots of people are people persons (say that five times fast). It doesn't leave anyone with an impression of who you really are. Think of how your statement might paint a more accurate picture.

Consider:

- I AM a crafty engineer.
- I AM a price negotiator.
- I AM a digital treasure hunter.
- I AM a fashionista.
- I AM a master of the kitchen.
- I AM a cat herder.

Each of those paint a clear picture of what you do or your skill sets. Feel free to use different ones to see which one people respond to best. Feel free to change your statement based on your audience.

After your I AM statement, you have your Value statement. This is your opportunity to summarize in one clear concise sentence ONE way that you add value to an organization. Of course you have many, a list of 20 in fact. However, pick one to really hone in on so people can get a clear picture of exactly what it is that you do that very few others can do. Again, consider what your audience (even if it is an audience of one) might respond to. You do not have to tell your whole story in this sentence, just enough to frame the conversation.

The intro (elevator pitch) that I use is:

> *Hello, My Name is Kim Brushaber. I'm the CEO of Bridge ATX. I am a connector. I connect individuals to Austin Businesses and businesses to the Austin Community.*

Notice that unless I speak VERY slowly, my intro takes less than 30 seconds. That's good because it allows me to give back that additional time to the person that I'm speaking to. Your intro allows people to get a basic understanding for what you do and allow the conversation to move forward.

Networking Story Telling

Once you've introduced yourselves to each other, it's time for the conversation to get started. Conversations will naturally flow based on commonalities between you and the other individual. However, I suggest that you start to figure out how to work in one of your top five stories into the conversation.

I have a very good friend of mine who frequently tells the story of how his name (which includes a SPAM word) gets caught in SPAM filters. This is a perfect opportunity for people to remember what his name is. Everyone gets a little laugh or giggle from it. Even though I've heard him tell it several times, it's still a very funny story. It is his ice breaker at events. It also helps people to remember his name.

I have another friend who has made a career transition from rocket scientist to attorney. Most people think that perhaps he's making a joke, when in fact he's telling the truth. People remember his story because very few of us have worked as a rocket scientist. They also remember that he's an attorney because it was such a drastic change in occupations.

While we can't all be comedians and we can't all have major career transitions, there is something interesting about every one of our lives. That's why ice breakers are used so frequently at networking events to get people talking to each other.

Think about your stories. Do you have a story that:

- Has a very funny outcome?
- Includes something that not many people have done?
- Includes a very impressive resolution?
- You are particularly proud of?

While you are out networking, consider what it is that your stories are telling people about you.

The last rule of networking stories is that you really should focus on getting a story's duration whittled down to two minutes or less. People have very short attention spans (especially at networking events). If you extend your story for too long, people will start to think about other things and get distracted by what's going on around the two of you instead of between the two of you. Try to make it a goal to pause every two minutes in your conversation. This will allow for a natural break in case either of you would like to move onto another conversation.

Telling Your Story on Your Resume

Lots of people have opinions on HOW you should write your resume. Every single person who looks at your resume will come up with ways to tweak it and change it. I'm not here to get into an argument over whether a Functional Resume or a Chronological Resume is better. However, I do believe there are some main points that apply to all resumes.

1) Can I spend 30 seconds and scan through a resume and find something that will capture my interest enough to prompt me to read more?
2) Can I quickly identify a person's skill set and the value they bring to a position?
3) Can I understand what is being said without having to read EVERY word?

I encourage everyone to do the 45 second resume review test. Give your resume to someone and set a time for 45 seconds. At the end of that time have them turn over your resume so that they can't see it. Have them tell you what they just read and what they understood from what was there. They will want to turn it back over to point out pieces; don't let them. It is valuable for you to understand "What is the first impression someone will walk away with from your resume?" After they have spilled out everything they can remember, you can then allow them to flip over your resume to provide you with more information. Do this with several people and see what kind of information people are retaining. You might also ask them to do a quick scan and tell you the first five things that jump out at them from your resume.

In order to make your resume more readable, I suggest you take these steps:

1) Put your strengths into phrases that are three words or less and create a bullet point section on your resume that includes your key strengths. Normally, I'll do this in a section that contains three even columns.
2) Review your BULLET POINTS from your Story, Action, Result template. Make sure that your favorite, most powerful bullet points are always included somewhere in your resume.
3) Based on the role that you are applying for – include all of the bullet points where your strength matches the strengths needed for the role.
4) Leave out any bullet points that do not directly apply to the position or do not showcase your top strengths (if submitting your resume via an online application).
5) Make sure that any applicable keywords associated with the position are included somewhere on your resume.

If you choose to use a chronological resume, be sure to put your bullet points in place based on where you exhibited that strength in that position. If you find that the number of bullet points for your positions are drastically unbalanced, go ahead and add in a few more bullet points for some of your other strengths.

Telling Your Story in the Interview

There are several different types of interviews – Information Gathering, Phone Screen, Face to Face, *etc*. For this discussion, I will assume that the interview is a hiring interview for a particular posted position. However, many of the discussion points in this section also apply to other types of interviews.

First, review the job description to determine what the company has said that they are looking for in an ideal match. If you don't have the job description, get as much information about the position from the referral source as possible.

1) Identify which of your strengths apply to what you believe they need for the position.
2) Identify which of your strengths apply to the bullet points indicated on the resume that you submitted for this position.
3) Create a "Topic List" for your interview.

Here's a partial "Topic List" that I might use:

Strength	Story	Position Held	Used in Interview
Networking	LinkedIn Contacts Tripled	STAFFING COMPANY – BDM	
Networking	Hosting Networking Events	Bridge ATX – CEO	
Networking	Network Like A Pro Classes	Bridge ATX – CEO	
Leadership	Teamwork Games	SOFTWARE COMPANY – App Support Team Lead	
Leadership	Executive Networking Group	Bridge ATX – CEO	
Training	Career Coaching Classes	Career Coaching Firm – Dir of Networking	
Training	Network Like A Pro Classes	Bridge ATX – CEO	
Training	Managing Director Networking Presentation	STAFFING COMPANY – BDM	

Feel free to create a "Topic List" that works for you.

Before the interview, make sure that any stories that you have indicated that you MIGHT tell are rehearsed with someone else. Be sure to time the stories and try to fit them in within a two minute window. Remember to keep the narrative part of the story down to a minute and a half saving 30 seconds for the action and result.

Remember that these are YOUR stories. There's nothing to get nervous about. No one else knows the story besides you. No one knows if you mess up whatever you have rehearsed. There is NO SCRIPT. Preparing for the stories in advance will help you to be able to flow more naturally when you are in the interview.

When you are in the interview, start to check off the stories that you have told. It's okay if you don't get to cover all of your stories. However, if you find that there is an entire strength section that has not been covered – be sure to ask them something like "I read in the job description that you are looking for someone who is very good at communicating with people. I would like the opportunity to elaborate on some of the points/questions you address in the interview. Would you like for me to share some additional stories of my strengths in that area? Or should I save that for a future conversation?"

Make sure that you also have a list of questions that you need to have answered. You might ask questions about the role and what it involves. You might ask questions to determine if the role will fit in your boundaries and your desired culture. You might ask about questions that apply to your reward system. Surprise, surprise - sometimes hiring decisions are made based on the person who asked the most relevant questions during an interview. This is where your pre-interview research will come in, but that's another conversation. For now, get started writing your stories and be prepared to brag yourself into your ideal next job/career/future.

Part Three: Convincing Someone to Hire You

In this third part of the workbook we're going to look at how to convince someone to hire you based on the story that you are able to tell them.

What Problem Do You Solve?

I find that many job seekers still don't know how to effectively express the problems that they solve for an organization. If you feel you are already an expert on your given field feel free to skip over the section on Discovery Meetings. I personally feel we always have more to learn.

I was talking to a friend of mine who is in marketing. I asked her what problems she solves for an organization. She rambled on for two or three minutes and I cut her off before she got to her point. With much love, I said, "That's boring and it doesn't tell me anything." She insisted that she wanted to tell me a story about what she had done in order to prove her point. Again, I cut her off (I know, I'm just mean and terrible). She wasn't giving me the ammo that I needed in order to help her find a job. In my head, I was thinking; "If I were at a networking event and I heard someone talking about a problem that they had with marketing in their company, would I think of her to solve it?" I don't know very much more than the average bear about marketing, so I really couldn't answer that question. Mostly I was just struggling to understand what she was saying to me and I wasn't really listening at all because I was just trying to understand. I stopped her again and said, "Tell me the problem that you solve so that a 6th grader could understand it." After a little more back and forth, we finally figured out the place where she added the most value was – "Most companies don't realize that there's a communications gap between marketing and sales – she is the person to identify the gap and fix it." Wow, now that's a powerful statement.

Creating that statement that simply allows me to listen for someone to say "My sales team and marketing team just aren't talking to each other." Bingo! My friend solves that problem. But even better, I can start a conversation from a small point of knowledge by saying "Do you know if your marketing team and sales team are communicating as effectively as they could be?" If the person that I am talking to is uncertain, then I can offer my friend up as a solution.

In fact, this same friend contacted me later about a position that she had applied for. I knew someone at that organization and asked about it. My friend at the company asked if I could recommend my marketing friend for the role (if so, he'd fast forward her resume). Because I had the conversation with my marketing friend, I knew where she shined in an organization and was able to pass that information along with my recommendation.

The exercise that we are going to work on now will help you get clarity on how you help an organization, based on Company Categories. Many job seekers have a variety of different paths that they can take based on their strengths and skill sets. However, these strengths and skill sets are used differently depending on the category that you are working within.

For example, let's say that three of my strengths are:

- Attention to Detail
- Requirements Gathering
- Inspiring People

These three strengths can be used in just about every organization. However, my passion may lie within these three focuses:

- Animal Rights
- Cooking
- Large International Organizations

In each of these categories there are problems within the organizations that can be solved by the strengths that I bring to the table.

In the case of Animal Rights, perhaps my attention to detail would be very helpful in organizing case loads as animal rights violations are reported. Perhaps my ability to gather requirements could be used in defining what the top ten perceived violations are and then clearly outlining why it's an issue and what can be done about it. Perhaps my ability to inspire people could be used to rally supporters in fundraising efforts.

In the case of Cooking, perhaps my attention to detail would be helpful in determining which quantities of ingredients are best combined together to get the most flavorful, fluffy cake. Perhaps my ability to gather requirements could be used to identify which menu items my clientele would enjoy the most at a restaurant. Perhaps my ability to inspire people could be used to get a group of people to show up for one of my cooking classes.

In the case of Large International Organizations, perhaps my attention to detail could be used to understand what is happening across the entire organization with the variety of projects that are being worked on. Perhaps my ability to gather requirements would allow me to be really good at understanding the various different cultures and customs across all of the different countries in the organization. Perhaps my ability to inspire people would allow me to overcome all of the different ways that the individual countries operate and inspire them to come together in one clear focus.

All of the strengths and skills that you have can easily be translated across multiple company categories. In order to focus yourself, you need to understand which company category groupings most interest you and then understand how your strengths can be used in those groupings to help the organizations within them.

[These charts need formatting help so they don't break across pages. More white space is good; the formatting changes should be part of the final proof, so I haven't tried any in this pass.]

Start by listing 10 Company Groupings that you might be interested in and then for the exercise below identify your top 3 to work with. These groupings can be based on industry, passion, size of company, stage of growth, or just about anything that interests you.

1)	
2)	
3)	
4)	
5)	
6)	
7)	
8)	
9)	
10)	

Next, you need to ponder what kinds of problems you think your chosen company category might have. Don't worry if it's wrong, it's just a starting point and you'll have an opportunity to refine it later via Discovery Meetings.

For Example:

Company Category

New Luxury Home Sales

Assumed Problem 1

Many loans are being foreclosed upon, which is making banks less likely to approve new home loans.

Assumed Problem 2

People are hunkering down due to the current economy and are not looking to invest in new luxury homes because they are afraid to take on new debt.

Assumed Problem 3

Foreigners who would typically buy new luxury homes are now looking at the US real estate market cautiously and are not buying new luxury homes at the moment.

Assumed Problem 4

People aren't able to sell their current homes, which keeps them from investing in new luxury homes.

Assumed Problem 5

People don't believe that the bottom has hit in the housing market and they are afraid that if they buy a new luxury home now, they will lose a lot of their gains in equity.

I don't work in this industry. Therefore, I don't know much about it other than what I see on the news. These are several of my assumptions of problems that this particular industry must be facing.

Based on the five problems above, if you were interested in getting into that industry, you would have to determine how (based on your past experience and my current passion) you can help to resolve some of those problems.

For problem #1 – You might be a great negotiator always finding great deals to close. You might be great at working with mortgage brokers to convince them to open up a deal for your clients.

For problem #2 – You might have some affluent clients who are looking to invest money in real estate who aren't bothered by taking on bad debt.

For problem #3 – You may be a native of Brazil and have a lot of clients who have been looking to purchase property in the US for a while now.

For problem #4 – You may be just as good at selling an existing home as you are at selling a new home and you might be able to help my clients sell their home in order to get them into the new dream home of their choice.

For problem #5 – You may have clients who don't care about the short term equity gain and are looking to retire and live for the next 20 years in a new custom home of their own design.

Now, let's try that with one of your company categories. Carefully review each of the assumed problems and see if you might be able to use your talents to solve some of their problems. If you don't know for sure, don't worry. This is just a starting point to frame your mind for the conversation.

Company Category 1 (Assumptions)
Assumed Problem 1
Assumed Problem 2
Assumed Problem 3
Assumed Problem 4
Assumed Problem 5

Company Category 1 (Solutions)
Solution for Assumed Problem 1
Solution for Assumed Problem 2
Solution for Assumed Problem 3

Solution for Assumed Problem 4
Solution for Assumed Problem 5

Company Category 2 (Assumptions)

Assumed Problem 1
Assumed Problem 2
Assumed Problem 3
Assumed Problem 4
Assumed Problem 5

Company Category 2 (Solutions)

Solution for Assumed Problem 1
Solution for Assumed Problem 2
Solution for Assumed Problem 3

Solution for Assumed Problem 4
Solution for Assumed Problem 5

Company Category 3 (Assumptions)

Assumed Problem 1
Assumed Problem 2
Assumed Problem 3
Assumed Problem 4
Assumed Problem 5

Company Category 3 (Solutions)

Solution for Assumed Problem 1
Solution for Assumed Problem 2
Solution for Assumed Problem 3

Solution for Assumed Problem 4
Solution for Assumed Problem 5

Discovery Meetings

Once you have an idea of the types of problems encountered in each of your company categories and you think you've identified solutions that you can bring to the table, it's time to start to prove your theories within the real world. The best way to do this is to start setting up Discovery Meetings.

Discovery Meetings are different from Informational Interviews. With a Discovery Meeting, you are there to talk to someone to get as much information from THEM as possible. You are not looking for how YOU fit into the picture. With an Informational Interview, you are exchanging information about the company as well as information about how you might be a fit for an organization. You should avoid letting a Discovery Meeting turn into an actual interview for a position. I know you're thinking "Wow, if only I had such problems," but trust me on this. Your goal in a Discovery Meeting is to remain neutral so that you can gather as much information as possible and keep the conversations flowing.

You don't have to stay in Discovery Meeting mode forever. Once you feel as though you have enough information about the problems that an organization has and what you do to solve those problems for them you can transition out of Discovery Meeting mode into Referral and Job Interview mode.

Discovery Meeting vs. Job Interview

Job Seekers get really excited when they are granted meetings with individuals within companies. Many times they have been looking at that black box of non-response. When someone will actually talk to them, the desperation can't be contained. I ask all of you to refrain from this behavior because it will KILL the process you are trying to work through.

If an individual hears that you are asking about a job, they will make a quick assessment on whether or not they think you would be a fit for the role. If you aren't a fit, the conversation ends, the door is closed, and things get a little uncomfortable. If you are a fit, then the individual will shuffle you off to HR and the hiring processes within the company. Either path kills the conversation for you.

Discovery Meetings are not about "the job" at all. They are about getting a better understanding for the industry and the company from a much broader sense. They are there to help you decide if it's an arena that you wish to work in. They are also there to help you to gather more insight and more information so that you can "dare people not to hire you" when the time is right. Discovery Meetings are more about the research, than the actual job.

Think of yourself as a lawyer trying to build a case. You would never see a lawyer talk about themselves when working on a case. They research all the information they can before a case goes to trial. During the trial, they ask questions from multiple people in order to build their case. Then at the end of the trial, when they feel they have done a good job of getting all the information they need, they bring everything back together and lead a jury to the verdict.

In this case, the verdict that you want is to get these individuals to hire you for a position. You can always go back and talk to these individuals later about a job (after you have gathered all the information). If there's no current position posted, you can go back later and plead your case to open one.

Many job seekers find themselves transitioning to a conversation about jobs during the discovery meeting process. DO NOT make the shift yourself or your request for a discovery meeting will seem like a false pretense and you will not receive any additional referrals for future discovery meetings. It will end the process right at that moment. Should the person you're talking to want to transition over to the conversation about a job, then feel free to allow the conversation to go in that direction if you feel you have already gathered the information that you seek. Just realize that making that decision ends the process, and you will have to start up the process again with someone else should you not be offered the job.

Who Should You Meet With

When you are first setting up your initial discovery meetings, the "who" is a little bit more challenging. Further into the process, you'll be given referrals to help you determine who you should be talking to. Until the referral process gets flowing, you will need to find people to meet with.

You can start with the contacts that you have identified for a company grouping. They were the first ones you thought of that related to that grouping. If you don't know anyone in a company grouping, marketing and sales individuals always seem to be the most willing to talk to people about what is going on in an industry. Try reaching out to them.

You should also look at who would be your boss in an organization. Look at an organization and find out who their competitors and vendors are, and meet with them. At the beginning, any information you can gather is helpful in starting the process. If you still can't find people to meet with, get out there to networking events and see if you can find individuals who can provide you input.

Asking for Help

Frequently, I meet with job seekers who are terrified to ask people to meet with them. They believe that they are wasting someone's time. Consider this scenario:

Someone approaches you and says "I am fascinated by <whatever you do>. I am in the process of interviewing people like you to learn more about <your work>. I would really like to learn more from someone with your expertise. Would you be willing to take a few moments to share your insight on this topic?"

If they genuinely meant it, would you meet with them? What if this person was referred to you by someone you know and trust? Most of us would; we enjoy having a captive listener appreciate our expertise. Some people would be suspicious because they aren't often asked for their opinion. Sincerity is the quickest way to clear up suspicion. How good would you feel having spent an hour with someone who really appreciates every second that you have given them?

After this conversation is over, you will know a bit more about this individual (although you would have done most of the talking). Imagine that you discover that this individual is a perfect candidate for a role that your best friend is trying to fill. Now you get to become the hero. The individual you talked to will appreciate you because you were the catalyst that led them to their next job. Your best friend will appreciate you because you supplied them with an amazing employee. Every single time you see either of them they will thank you for the connection that you have made. That connection would not have been possible without you. How good would that feel?

In meeting with these individuals, you have the opportunity to give them these gifts. It isn't a burden to them if you approach it from the right angle. Sincerity is the key to doing that. You know that if the shoe were on the other foot you would do the same thing for them (or I would at least hope you would, having gone through this experience yourself).

Just make sure that it is easy for them to meet with you and have this discussion.

Additionally, you should consider how easy it is for an individual to help you. If I were to ask a friend to pick me up at the airport at 2 PM on a Saturday, most of my friends would be more than happy to help me as long as they were not already doing something. A smaller group of my friends would be willing to pick me up at the airport at 2 AM. An even smaller group of friends (perhaps only family) would be willing to bail me out of jail at 2 AM.

The easier it is for someone to help you the more comfortable they will be and the more success you'll have in gaining their assistance. If the task is a more difficult one, then the better they know you the more likely they will come to your aid.

In order to make it easier you should:

1) Make the request easy to understand
2) Indicate why it is that you need the help
3) Indicate what they stand to gain by helping you

Humans are inclined to help one another. Sometimes people do like to play the Godfather and call in favors. Most of them will be more than willing to help to make introductions during a job search if they have a clear understanding of the value that both parties will receive during the job search. Additionally, most people will be willing to talk to you if they believe that you are genuinely interested in what they have to say.

The Four Levels of Discovery Meetings

Level 1 – You haven't had any discussions yet on the industry/grouping. Everything is guesswork. You are simply looking to gather some information from a contact and you are hoping that that contact can help you to connect to other people who can give you more information.

Level 2 – You've had your initial conversations on the industry/grouping. You have some information and insight into what's going on with it. You have a better understanding of the problems that face that industry/grouping. You can talk to the contact on a level with a greater understanding of what is going on and you can start to see some solutions forming for the problems that they face.

Level 3 – You have a good understanding of what is going on in the industry/grouping. You can talk about the industry/grouping from a place of knowledge. You are able to offer input on the industry/grouping that the contact may not be aware of. You can talk about both the problems within the industry/grouping as well as the potential solutions.

Level 4 - You have a solid understanding of what is going on in the industry/grouping. You offer insightful solutions to the problems that hamper the industry/grouping. People are looking to you as a subject matter expert on the topic of that industry/grouping. You are confident about your level of knowledge and expertise. You know how to provide the solution and are available to the highest bidder. People seek you out.

It is possible that you might meet with one particular contact at each of the levels in the Discovery Meeting process. Don't think that just because you met with someone at Level 1 that you can't circle back and talk to them again when you have hit Level 2.

If you already have a lot of knowledge regarding your industry/grouping, it is possible that you could enter discussions at a Level 2 or Level 3. That's okay; you don't have to start at a Level 1 for every company grouping.

There is no preset number that tells you that you should move from one level to another level. It's all about your comfort with the subject matter. It might take you two meetings to go from a Level 1 to a Level 2 and it might take you eight.

My Discovery Meetings with Austin Gaming Companies

In order to help you to understand the benefits of Discovery Meetings a little better, allow me to share my experiences when I was gaining knowledge about the Gaming Industry in Austin, Texas.

I was working for a large recruiting company. I had identified that there were fifty gaming studios in Austin and my recruiting company was not working with any of them. I thought that this was a greatly untapped resource. I thought that if I could gain knowledge about the industry I would have a leg up on any competition that I might encounter.

For Level 1, I heard that there was a gaming networking event going on. I attended the event and approached all of the panelists after the conversation was over. I told them that I was fascinated by games and the gaming industry and I wanted to learn more about it. I was hoping that they might be able to share time with me to tell me more about gaming in Austin. Three of them agreed.

So, I went and met with each of them. I explained I was a newcomer and I wanted to know whatever they could tell me within an hour. I did tell them I wanted to frame the question around what it takes to find a good hire in the industry, since that was my focus. Each of them sat patiently with me and explained their perspective. From those three conversations, I was able to piece together the similarities of what each of them said, as well as challenges that were different amongst the conversations.

For Level 2, I asked for a conversation with some of the people in charge of hiring at the gaming studios. In fact, one studio was throwing a huge hiring event and I showed up just to get a feel for the environment. Besides the people who worked there, I was the only person in the room not looking for a job. So it allowed people to be more relaxed and talk more freely around me. I was able to use a little of the understanding that I had gained at Level 1 to be able to talk to them from a more knowledgeable standpoint about what was going on within their industry. They confirmed the same issues that I had heard from the other people I had met with.

As I continued to meet with the hiring managers, I was quickly able to identify one of the major pain points in regards to hiring game studio talent in Austin, Texas. There was no one out there who really had their finger on the pulse of what talent was available in Austin. The traditional recruiting firms that they were working with were sending them talent from the East Coast and West Coast, but no one knew the talent in Austin. I quickly realized that I had a leg up on my competition because I was on the street in Austin and had the capability to start meeting all of the interested local talent.

So, that propelled me into Level 3. I started to meet with everyone. I was able to tell studios about the things that were happening at other studios. I knew who was growing and who was shrinking. I knew about their game release dates and how they affected their hiring schedules. I knew what talent was available and when they were available. I became friends with a lot of these people. I understood them.

That caused me to slingshot pretty quickly into Level 4. I was just an email or phone call away from knowing all the talent in the Austin area. Did I know everyone? Absolutely - not. However, I had identified key contributors in a variety of organizations all across town. You don't have to know everything if you know all the people who know everything.

While I wasn't looking for a job, I was still looking for someone to hire me to help them with their hiring processes, which really isn't a whole lot different from what job seekers are doing every day.

You might say "Oh sure, you're just an extrovert. You don't have problems talking to anyone." While that may be true, it doesn't mean that you can't do what I have done.

Discovery Meeting Referrals (1-2-3)

Building up a list of people to meet with and grow your knowledge is just a matter of math. Each time you have a meeting with someone, you should wrap up the conversation with a statement like:

"I really enjoyed talking to you today. Now that we've had a chance to speak with each other, I think you have a better understanding of the kind of information that I am looking to gather. Do you have three people that you might be able to refer me to so that I can continue this conversation?"

Not everyone is going to be able to come up with three people. If you only get one person, the lines of communication stay open and you have another conversation available to build your knowledge.

Ask your contact if it's better for you to reach out to the referral or if it's better for them to do it on your behalf. Different people have different levels of comfort in how they handle their contact list. If they would like to contact their referral first, make sure to suggest that you could write an email that highlights why you'd like to talk to the referral so that it's easier for your contact to forward the request along. The easier you can make it on your contact the better success you'll have in getting the next meeting set up.

Make sure that you also ask why the person/people they have suggested would be good to meet with. It's a great way to frame the conversation when you are requesting a meeting with them. For example:

"Hello Matt –

I'm so glad that Jimmy was willing to introduce us. He was helpful when I was talking to him about the changes that are happening in Green Energy. After our conversation, he suggested that I should talk to you about your perspective on what is happening in the solar energy field. He believes that you are a subject matter expert in that field right now and that there's no one better for me to talk to. If you have thirty minutes next week, I would love to have the opportunity to come and talk to you and gather your insight on this topic of conversation.

Here are a few questions I was considering asking you ……"

The Math behind the Referral System

The math starts to look a little something like this:

Take the top three connected people you know in a particular company category. Let's say that two of them give you three more people to meet with and one only gives you one:

3 + 3 + 1 = 7 new meetings

From those seven new meetings, you can quickly level up to a Level 2 (or maybe 3). Let's say that a few of them give you one or two and maybe some give you three referrals:

1 + 1 + 1 + 2 +2 + 3 + 3 = 13 new meetings

With those thirteen meetings, if you're asking the right questions you're up to Level 4. It's possible that people will start to refer you back in places that you might have already been referred. So, some of them won't pan out to any referrals but some will.

0 + 0 + 0 + 0 + 1 + 1 + 1 + 1 + 2 + 2 + 2 + 3 + 3 = 16 new meetings

From this example, the three initial contacts who gave you a variety of referrals, you ended up with thirty-nine meetings with different contacts. If you end up circling back after you've gained all that knowledge, then it's thirty nine opportunities for people to hire you. Just be sure to keep asking for those referrals and go to all the meetings that people are nice enough to set up for you.

Let's run the example that you started with 3 people and through the 4 levels they each referred you to 2 new people you would have:

3 * 2 = 6 (level 2)
6 * 2 = 12 (level 3)
12 * 2 = 24 (level 4)

3 + 6 + 12 + 24 = 45 meetings

Do you think that you could become a subject matter expert on this topic after having 45 meetings?

The reality is that you probably won't need that many meetings in order to accomplish your goal. In fact you could probably complete your Discovery Meetings within 10 – 15 meetings. Each person you talk to is going to make you better equipped to walk into a room and dare someone not to hire you for a role. Additionally, each person you talk to is someone that you can go back to once you have gathered all your information when you are prepared to ask for a job.

It's up to you to decide if you want to approach discovery meetings in your top three company categories at the same time. Some people have the capacity to easily switch between the conversations. Some people need to just focus in on one area at a time. Do whatever works for you. If you feel a slowing in the process for one of your company groupings, be sure to start propelling meetings into your other company groupings as well.

The purpose of Discovery Meetings is to help you to build expertise on a subject and to allow you to decide whether or not you want to take on the new opportunities that you seek.

Discovery Meeting Questions

You should always know in advance the questions that you'd like to ask at each level of the Discovery Meeting conversations. When you request a meeting, it's always good to let the other person know what kind of questions you will be asking in order to frame the conversation appropriately.

Level 1: Questions should be very vague, because, at that point, you really don't have much information about the company category yet.

Some good questions are:

1) What made you decide to work in this industry/grouping?
2) What are your favorite parts of your job?
3) If you could go back in time before you started this job, what would you tell yourself?
4) What can you tell me about this industry/grouping?
5) My understanding of this industry/grouping is that one of your biggest problems may be
   _____. Is this true? Can you help me to understand better?
6) What is the biggest issue facing this industry/grouping right now?
7) If a good friend of yours wanted to join this industry/grouping, what would you persuade them to do or not to do?

Make sure to rank which questions you'd like to have answered first. It is possible that you may only get to one or two questions in the conversation depending on how talkative the other person is or how much time they have available to talk to you. Be prepared to have more questions available in case conversation dies down, but chances are you will never get to your fifth question.

Level 2: Questions should be geared more towards the things that you have learned about the grouping/industry. It's your opportunity to show them that you do have a little knowledge on the topic while still respecting the other person's perspective on things. Be prepared for them to offer you a perspective that you might not have encountered yet. Make sure your questions are not too opinionated or biased. You are not the expert in this arena yet. Be open to their perspectives.

Some questions might look like:

1) While researching this industry/grouping, I have discovered that _____. I would love to hear more about your perspective on this topic.
2) I'm starting to hear that this industry/grouping seems to encounter issues regarding _____. What is your opinion on how these issues are affecting your industry/grouping?
3) How do you think that someone could best solve the issues facing this industry/grouping at this time?

Of course, you can always throw in questions from the Level 1 choices in order to get them to open up, talk more about themselves, and become comfortable with you.

Level 3: Questions are from a much greater place of knowledge. At this point you should have a variety of different perspectives on the industry/grouping that you are focusing in on. However, you must still remember that you are seeking information from the other person. You must still be all ears to the input that they have. There should be a point where you can have more of a conversation, than just asking one-sided questions.

While you can still plan to use the questions that you have prepared for Level 1 and Level 2, you will find that the conversation will open up much wider. This will allow the conversation to lead you toward follow up questions based on the discussion at hand. I encourage you to have questions handy in case the conversation dies down. At this point you should really be focusing in on letting the conversation flow naturally.

You can also use Level 3 Discovery Meetings as a sounding board to see if the solutions that you have been swirling in your head will be effective solutions for them. Give away the "What" for free, but sell them the "How." The devil is in the details.

Level 4: Questions should be even less of a "question" than any of the previous conversations. By this point it should be much more of a back and forth banter and exchanging of ideas. This is the point where you can showcase the knowledge that you've gathered, as well as convince them to hire you for your solutions.

Discovery Meeting Format

While Level 3 and Level 4 Discovery Meetings are much more "dialog-oriented", it can be difficult to know what to do when you are starting in at a Level 1 or Level 2 "question-oriented" meeting.

I suggest that you should follow this format for a one hour meeting for a Level 1 or Level 2 conversation:

First 5 Minutes – Introductions, Small Talk, and Finding Commonalities
05 Minutes – 10 Minutes – Frame the Conversation (Discuss what you will be discussing)
10 Minutes – 40 Minutes – Ask Your Questions and Gather Responses
40 Minutes – 50 Minutes – Ask if there is anything you might be able to do to help them
50 Minutes – 60 Minutes – Summarize Next Steps, Ask For Referrals, Thank You

Introductions, Small Talk, and Finding Commonalities

For the first five minutes, you'll introduce yourself and try to start making each other comfortable. Look around the room and see if there's anything you have in common. If you were referred to them by someone, you might bring the other person up. It's your opportunity to get the other person to loosen up a little to talk to you. Make sure to keep the conversation on a professional level (unless you know them on a personal level).

Frame the Conversation

For the next five minutes, you'll frame the conversation with them so that they understand how the conversation will flow. This allows you to better facilitate the conversation so that there are no hard feelings if you have to cut the conversation a little bit short. You do not have to be a stickler on the time clock. If you spend all your time focused on the clock, then you are not listening to what the other person has to say.

Ask Your Questions and Gather Responses

For the next thirty minutes, you should open the conversation up to the questions that you have come prepared to ask. Realize that, depending on how talkative the individual is, you may be limited in the number of questions you can ask them.

Ask if You Can Help Them

When there is a natural pause in the conversation (typically when there are about 15 to 20 minutes left in the conversation) you should ask them how you might be able to help them. They have taken the time to talk to you, you should see if there's some way you can repay the favor. Sometimes, their request is something that you can do right then (for example, they might like to have a conversation with someone you have already talked to). Sometimes it is a request for you to gather some information for them in future conversations. If you can't find a way to help them (now or in the future), that's okay. The fact that you honestly made the gesture to help is good enough.

Summarize and Ask For Referrals

For the last 5 to 10 minutes of the conversation, you should go over the next steps from the conversation. If they have promised to do something for you (like introduce you to someone or provide you with information), let them know you will be following up with them later regarding that request. If you have promised to do something for them, make sure that you have set up a time frame when you can do that for them. This is also the time to ask them for referrals. If they have enjoyed the conversation they may have plenty of people for you to talk to. If not, they might be limited in the help that they chose to provide. Any help or any information that they give you should be greatly appreciated. Make sure to thank them for their time.

Discovery Meeting Follow Up

Upon completion of the meeting, you should send them a "Thank You" for their time via email or a note card. I had a friend of mine who used to pre-address an envelope before she went to meet with anyone. Whenever she'd get back to the car after her conversation she would write a small note and drop it in the mail. This was above and beyond (and sincerely appreciated), so you don't have to do that. You should reach out to them in some manner, within a few days of the meeting, to thank them for their time.

It's also appropriate, when you are thanking them, to remind them of any action items that they have said that they would take. If they don't respond back within a few days, give them the option to gently back out on their commitments. Sometimes, people over commit what they are capable of in the heat of a conversation (especially if drinks are involved) and, upon reflection, they can't deliver. This is not always the case, but it is nice to be gracious, just in case.

If there is anything that you have said you would do, you should take action on those items as soon as you possibly can. People are more likely to help eager responsive people. If there is an action to be taken after your action (for example you may write a note that they can forward onto one of their contacts), then time is of the utmost importance in order to ensure a quick turnaround for your request.

If you have promised to do something at a later point in time (like gather information over the course of your later conversations), make sure to follow up as soon as you have that information for them.

If you have met with someone that your contact has referred, you should follow up with an email (or note) after that meeting to thank your original contact for making the connection that allowed you to further your conversation. This is also a good time to ask them if they have thought of anyone else who would be useful for you to talk to.

Discovery Meeting Keys to Success

Here are some key things to remember for successful discovery meetings:

- Always be respectful of anyone who agrees to meet with you
- Always maintain a sense of professionalism
- Follow up quickly
- Thank your contacts for any help that they have provided to you
- Be respectful of people's time when they meet with you (don't be the one to run over)
- Plan your questions in advance, so your questions can be answered
- Don't let the conversation get to "job" until you are at Level 3 or above in your meeting levels

If you follow this process, you will find that you quickly become the knowledge expert on the company grouping that you have identified to research. This allows you to have better knowledge about all of their problems and exactly what you can do within an organization to step in and help them out. At this point, it really comes down to presenting them with their problem, getting them to accept that it is their problem, and then discussing how much they are willing to pay to make that problem go away.

Along this path you should also be able to clearly see which of the organizations in each company grouping are ones that you would most enjoy working for. This adds a further level of passion regarding both the role and the company.

Remember in these conversations not to turn the Discovery Meetings into a job interview. Also, when you are in these conversations as "the expert," tell them what you would do to resolve the issue, but save the how for when they pay you for it.

Building Up Steam with Referrals

At this point you can transition from Discovery Meeting to Job Discussion. The next natural step in the process is to find referrals. Referrals can start from friends and family but they can also start with Internal Champions, Headhunters and Recruiters. The key is to get around the automated process and start talking and interacting with people.

As noted above in the Discovery Meeting section, referrals can build quickly if you get in the habit of asking each person you meet with if they wouldn't mind referring you to 2 – 3 other people.

Differentiating Yourself

I run a weekly conversation for executive job seekers. Each week I have them introduce themselves to the group based on their functional area and how they add value to an organization. Frequently I hear individuals within the group describe themselves the same way as another person in the group. As a recruiter, I don't know how to tell the two of them apart. To me it sounds like they are competing for exactly the same roles. The reality is that they probably are. If I am a Hiring Manager, how am I going to decide between them when there is only one role to be filled?

I also frequently hear about job seekers who can get a lot of interviews and often find themselves in the running as one of the top three candidates for a given role. However, these individuals continually come back to me and say that they did not get selected. How is it that over and over again they are the final contenders, but they do not achieve their end goal of being the victor?

In both of these cases, the issue is that the individual is not clearly differentiating themselves from the pack. While it is true that making yourself stand out may make you the one who is not selected, more often than not it is that clear differentiation that allows you to become selected. That extra feather in your cap is why you are not only just as good as the other candidates in the running but that you are better.

In this workbook, we have already worked extensively on defining your strengths. You should now have an understanding of how those strengths can be used in an organization. These are all essential parts in convincing someone that they need to hire you for the role.

So now the question becomes how do you go from being a fit to the being the perfect fit? You must know what your special feather in your cap is that everyone else who has ever held that role does not have.

I'll give you an example:

I was working with a job seeker I'll refer to as Michael. Upon reviewing his resume, I saw that he was clearly a very good product development manager. He had metrics and statistics that spoke to all of his strengths and what he could accomplish. Comparing his resume to the job description, he would always be a perfect fit. When Michael described himself, there was never a question about who he was, what he did and how he added value to an organization. This man had it all wrapped up in a neat little bow, and yet he still wasn't able to clear that final hurdle of being selected for the positions he was interviewing for. In some cases he was able to identify the individuals who were selected over him. When I asked him why they were selected over him he didn't have an answer. He couldn't identify a skill set that they had that he didn't. You might think, "well they just liked the other guy more," except that it happened over and over and over again.

So I asked Michael what made him different from the other guys. His response? "Nothing.", I pointed out to him therein lay his entire problem. Nothing made him different or made him standout from any other skilled and highly qualified development manager. He had everything he needed to do the jobs with his eyes blindfolded and hands tied behind his back.

I started working with Michael to see if we could identify beyond the job description what he did differently that no other development manager he has ever worked with could do as well as him. After a long conversation we discovered that Michael genuinely cared about his entire team. He knew details about them like their family, their hobbies and all of their strengths. He truly enjoyed sitting with these individuals and mentoring them to identify where their career path should follow. He cared about them so much that sometimes he would coach his team out of the roles they were working in so that they could follow their true passion. Being a career coach, of course I could relate to what he was doing and why it was so special to find a manager who had this talent. This led him to always be surrounded with a loyal team who was happy and overly productive.

Michael didn't realize that what he was doing was different from anyone else. He was just being himself and playing to his strengths. I pointed out that not only was he a very good development manager but that he was essential to the organizations that he worked with because of his ability to mentor, inspire, and motivate his team.

The next interview that Michael had, he went in and addressed all of the points that were necessary to allow the company to understand that he had everything necessary in order to work in the role that they were hiring for. However, this time in the final interview he was able to also bring out his ability to rally his team around him and explain how this was essential for an organization.

Interestingly, in this interview he did not get the role. This was because the organization that he was interviewing with did not see the value in having good mentors. Instead, they viewed everyone as an interchangeable asset that could be replaced at any time. None of the conversations up until that point had shown any light on this situation. He learned that he did not want to work for an organization that could not appreciate this special skill that he brought to the table. He would have never been able to use it effectively in that environment.

The next opportunity came up and he went into the interview. This time, when he presented his special talent for team building, the organization was overjoyed. They started asking him how he implemented his techniques and how he was able to motivate so many different types of developers (developers are a rare breed; I know because I used to be one). This time, he overcame the final hurdle and was chosen for the job. He has never been happier to be in an organization that is so supportive of him and as the unique skills he brings as a manager.

Now that you have gone through all of your strengths and have defined how you are a fit for an organization, I want you to think about what are those final feathers in your cap that you have that no one else in that role has. The secret to finding these feathers typically resides in the things that you are most passionate about outside of work. These are the things at the end of the day, after your job has been done, that you can feel really good about.

Let's start by taking a role that you are pursuing.

ROLE TITLE -

Now list the top 5 things that anyone who works in this role should be able to do. This can be pulled from your knowledge of the role OR you can pull it from the consistent things that are written in job descriptions for this role.   Unless this is a brand new role for you, you should find that you can also do these 5 things very well.

1)	
2)	
3)	
4)	
5)	

Now think about 3 additional things that you can to add value to the role that are rarely seen on a job description for this role. If you don't know, refer back to your strengths or ask for help.

1)	
2)	
3)	

These 3 things are the feathers in your cap. Because you enjoy them and are naturally good at them, they will likely come out in some form or fashion during all stages of your interview. However, it is essential in that final interview that you make sure that you have covered how you can perform the first 5 talents and then also work in the additional 3 talents that you have that are different. This will make or break you in the selection process. If you are chosen, you will know that you have found the right new home.

The End of the Story

With a little help from your friends you should now have the lines of your dream job drawn. You should be able to define your:

- Loves
- Strengths
- Boundaries
- Reward System
- Ideal Culture

However, the most important part is that you now know how to tell your story so that you can go out and convince someone to hire you for that position.

After that, it is essential that you set up Discovery Meetings in order to validate that what you are dreaming about doing is what you actually want to do.

While this is not everything you need for your whole job search journey, it is the very first building block to identifying your dream job and helping you to get it.

Good Luck Out There!

Identifying Your Dream Job

IDENTIFYING YOUR DREAM JOB

And Telling Your Story to Get It

APPENDIX

Appendix A: Transformation – Career Transition

What follows is a real-life scenario. A good friend of mine was hoping to transition from a salon job where she has worked her whole career into something else. She wasn't sure how her skills and strengths might apply to any other type of work and came to me for help.

We started to work together and discovered that these are her LOVES:

- AHA Moments
- Animals
- Customer Service/Retail/Public
- Excitement
- Finding Alternative Mutually Beneficial Solutions
- Mixers/Networking
- Music
- Preparing Facts
- Rallying People
- Teaching New Knowledge
- Working with People

These are her STRENGTHS:

- Balancing Personalities
- Collaboration
- Delegation
- Deriving People's Wants/Needs
- Deriving the Truth
- Diffusing Situations
- Empathy
- Handling Drama
- Honesty and Truthfulness
- Listening/Hearing
- Managing Monkeys (teams of up to 24 people)
- Planning/Scheduling
- Recruiting and Retaining Talent
- Working With the Public

These are her BOUNDARIES ((D) indicates a Deal Breaker):

- Believe in Product/Service (D)
- Benefits (D)
- Closer to Home
- Fun
- Guilt Free
- Job Security (no Paranoia/Pins and Needles/Brown Nosing) (D)
- Less Stressful

- One Direct Report
- Personal Recognition (D)
- Standing All Day
- Travel
- Truthful Environment
- Typing

We started to go through her stories and discovered that she has accomplished a lot of very cool things over the course of her career. Rather than show you her stories for this example, I thought I would just show you what her revised resume ended up looking like once we were done.

These are the Skills and Expertise Sections from her Original Resume:

Skills

- Personnel Management / Training
- Customer Relations
- Merchandising
- Store Design / Set-Up
- Inventory Control
- Advertising / Selling Techniques
- Cash Management / Budget Control
- Forecasting
- Hair Stylist

Expertise

- Development of ongoing client relationships with individual attention to detail, creating loyal customer following
- Comprehensive, broad based knowledge of all aspects of business ownership and retail store management
- Scheduling, inventory, payroll, guest services
- Retail ordering, inventory control promotions and advertising
- Planning and implementation of merchandise presentation
- Natural fashion ability; easily recognizing upcoming style expressions and profitable ideas/situations
- Facilitated successful completion of local fashion shows utilizing one hundred plus models and business participants
- Seasonal attendance of high profile New York Trade and Fashion Shows
- Bi-yearly fashion photo layouts in weekly newspaper
- All aspects of customer service, as well as visual merchandising
- Performed full personal service, retained eighty-five percent client base
- Managed staff of twenty plus

This is what her revised resume became:

___

Skills

- Advertising / Marketing
- Budgeting and Forecasting
- Conflict Resolution
- Customer Relations

- Delegation
- Honesty / Loyalty / Truthfulness
- Inventory Control
- Personnel Management

- Problem Solving
- Recruiting and Retaining Talent
- Scheduling/Planning
- Store Design / Layout

Expertise

- Exceeded corporate goals by combining individual personal employee needs to match company goals *resulting in 85% of employees meeting or exceeding all of their goals*
- Implemented creative alternative workspace solutions *resulting in 25% increase in revenue*
- Won the "Club of Excellence" award for increasing growth, revenue and retention and decreasing cost for 3 years in a row which was a feat unsurpassed by anyone else in the 5,000+ person company
- Recruited and Retained Talent *resulting in 100% retention* over the course of a year in an industry that averages 60% turnover during the same duration
- Staffed and trained entire salon in 9 locations that went on to become award winning locations
- Anticipated needs of upcoming sales cycles when ordering inventory *resulting in being fully stocked 98% of the time*
- Managed and maintained schedules of 20 commission based and 5 hourly based employees
- Maintained client base of over 100 decade long clients
- Participated in a variety of events benefiting charities such as St Baldrick's, Safe Place, Susan G Komen Foundation and the American Cancer Society
- Orchestrated every aspect of a professional photo shoot with the exception of actually taking the picture
- Interacted professionally with over 500 people on a weekly basis
- Resolved over 50 customer issues on a weekly basis with win-win results for all parties

As you can see, her resume still applies to the job that she has done so well over the course of her career. However, because she has now accented her strengths, people can start to understand how those strengths might also apply to their business instead of just the salon industry.

If some of these strengths do not apply to a position she is considering, she can simply take out those particular bullet points.

Appendix B: Transformation – Converting a Negative Situation

A friend came to me because she was struggling with how to transform a negative situation into a positive story. Originally, when she created her resume she tried to play it very safe with her bullet points so none of the negativity came through. However, when we started working through her story she started to see that she actually had some very positive outcomes from the situation.

This is a section of her resume BEFORE she went through the Story Telling process:

<DATE>, General Manager of North American Operations, <COMPANY>
- Promoted to General Manager of North American Operations due to outstanding performance
- Sold and delivered energy management and energy prepayment programs and technology
- Grew customer base by over 100% throughout US, Canada and the Caribbean
- Led sales efforts including direct sales, channel sales and distributor co-marketing programs
- Instrumental in defining requirements and specifications for new product lines
- Created launch strategy for next generation SmartGrid system with a $10M first year revenue goal
- Managed the transition of all US operations to the UK office before being laid off

After going through the process with me, she uncovered these stories:

STRENGTH
Rebalancing Expectations
STORY
CEO announced a product release date of an upcoming product without taking development cycles into account. Distributors started to pre-sell the system before its official release date, but were promising the release date as firm to customers. Development slipped and updated information was released to the channel, however, some distributors continued to promise the original release date, then referenced back to the CEO presentation as reason for not complying with new information. I reissued the launch press release and other materials to update positioning w/more ambiguous timing information. Distributor continued to provide original release date and other unsubstantiated product feature set information to customers.
ACTION
After a channel reorganization, I assessed customer expectations with regards to the upcoming availability and function of our promised next generation system. I then realigned expectations and devised an ongoing customer communication and care plan.
RESULT
Retained 60% of at-risk customers while improving customer satisfaction by 50% and while growing total customer base by 91%
BULLET POINT
Assessed customer expectations after restructuring activities, realigned expectations and devised an on-going customer care and communications plan. Retained 60% of at-risk customers while growing total customer base by 91%.

Another example story from our conversation:

STRENGTH
Holding People Accountable
STORY
Inherited a dysfunctional distributor channel with a primary distributor who did not provide information in a timely or reliable manner, causing confusion and unmet expectations for both the company and its end customers. In addition to supplying poor information about key operations (forecasts, delivery schedules, customer requirements, etc.), the distributor also misrepresented the brand to the market (features and commercial availability) and withheld funds owed in an attempt to build leverage and influence corporate deliverables and product strategy.
ACTION
During my initial tenure with the company, I introduced new processes to reduce the return merchandise backlog, better forecast upcoming sales orders and delivery dates and review account status monthly. After some improvement, the distributor returned to their past bad behavior. To terminate continued counterproductive behavior, I worked with corporate leadership to end the distributor relationship and bring in new representation.
RESULT
Recaptured $200k in additional revenue during the next 10 months in this open territory.
BULLET POINT
Assessed and revamped reseller channel structure and processes in order to realign partner performance with corporate objectives. Reclaimed additional $200k revenue in the next 10 months.

Her Resume transformed to look like this:

GM, North American Customer Operations, <COMPANY> Austin, TX   <DATE>

Directed customer engagement activities (marketing/sales, contract negotiations, project deployment and after-sale support) with utilities across Canada, the US, Mexico and the Caribbean for this $5M energy-management and prepayment technology/services portfolio of a UK-based division. Fostered interaction and managed relationships with C- and director-level decision makers and project teams.

- Assessed and revamped reseller channel structure and processes in order to realign partner performance with corporate objectives. Reclaimed additional $200k revenue in the next 10 months.

- Assessed customer expectations after restructuring activities, realigned expectations and devised an on-going customer care and communications plan. Retained 60% of at-risk customers while growing total customer base by 91%.

- Hired, on-boarded and mentored US-based technical support engineer. This initiative contributed to a 50% increase in customer satisfaction and relieved UK staff to focus on product development work.

- Re-launched brand 3X due to company name changes and conducted a soft re-launch of next generation system. By sustaining high divisional visibility, shortened a 2-year sale cycle to 10 months.

Appendix C: Transformation – Multiple Stories for the Same Strength

When discussing stories with this friend, we started to uncover that she was really good at getting in and doing the same thing over and over again. So, while creating the stories did not yield very many new bullet points it did help her to have a slate of stories that she could tell regarding each bullet point on her resume.

This is a section of her resume BEFORE she went through the Story Telling Process:

<COMPANY NAME> Austin, Texas <DATES>

Sales Manager, CENTRAL REGION

- Implemented software across multiple sites for global customers.
- Increased revenue growth for major accounts.

Here are two abbreviated stories pertaining to "Salvaging a Broken Relationship" where the resulting bullet point ended up exactly the same.

STRENGTH
Salvaging a Broken Relationship
STORY
Previously there was a bad relationship with our customer due to their experience with my company before I started to work there. I had a personal connection and by talking with them, they finally agreed to meet with me to discuss the company. I took them to lunch to discover the problems that they had in the past – "truth finding."I determined where we could correct the behavior. I assured them that we now have a new team in town. I was able to get them to trust me to deliver what I promised.
ACTION
Reestablished integrity and trust with one of our major customers
RESULT
They agreed to meet with me regarding setting up a new deal
BULLET POINT
Salvaged a broken relationship with one of our major customers resulting in negotiations to start a new contract

STRENGTH
Salvaging a Broken Relationship
STORY
A gatekeeper at one of our customers was in charge of Engineering. The door was closed to us due to several communication break downs. I started building a relationship with his personal assistant. I negotiated for 30 minutes of his time. I made the assistant feel like she was the most important person in order for me to get on his scheduled. In the meeting I determined where we could correct past behavior.
ACTION
Reestablished integrity and trust with one of our major customers
RESULT

They agreed to meet with me regarding setting up a new deal
BULLET POINT
Salvaged a broken relationship with one of our major customers resulting in negotiations to start a new contract

Here are two abbreviated about being a "Closer" which resulted in the same bullet point.

STRENGTH
Closer
STORY
We had an existing relationship with a client. I met with them and showed them the new technology. I discovered what problems they were trying to solve with the products. I came up with a solution with our products which was workable and could bring them ahead in the product. I showed them the ROI to save millions of dollars a year.
ACTION
Delivered a custom made solution to a major customer's problem
RESULT
2 Year Contract for $2M that saved the customer millions of dollars a year
BULLET POINT
Delivered a custom made solution for a major customer resulting in a 2 year contract for $2M that saved the customer several million dollars a year

STRENGTH
Closer
STORY
I met with the engineering team in Japan to show them our technology and why we stand out. Because this engineering team had a different cultural background than we did in the US, I was extra sensitive to their needs and ways of doing business. Other companies who had addressed the team did not factor in their cultural differences. I determined what problems they were having, customized the solution to solve their problem and presented them with a solution that they could easily take to their executive team.
ACTION
Delivered a custom, solution to a major customer's problem
RESULT
1 year Contract for $800K that saved the customer several million dollars a year
BULLET POINT
Delivered a custom made solution for a major customer resulting in a one year contract for $800K that saved the customer several million dollars a year

In all four examples, the stories have been slightly abbreviated for the sake of anonymity. However, even from the abbreviated examples you can start to see the power that has come from those stories. For two separate strengths she had two separate stories which yielded almost identical results for her customers. Having both stories available to her in an interview she could provide solid examples of how she is able to repeat this behavior over and over again.

Her resume would now include these new bullet points:

<COMPANY NAME> Austin, Texas *<DATES>*

Sales Manager, CENTRAL REGION
- Salvaged multiple broken relationship with several of our major customers resulting in negotiations to start new contracts worth $5M
- Delivered a custom made solution for several major customer resulting in new contracts worth $4M that saved our customer several million dollars a year

In an interview, when she is asked to explain each bullet point she can confidently say she has two different examples of how she was able to arrive at that outcome for each point.

Appendix D: Create Your Own Transformations

Story, Action, Result Template

STRENGTH

STORY

ACTION

RESULT

POSITION HELD

BULLET POINT

Story, Action, Result Template

STRENGTH

STORY

ACTION

RESULT

POSITION HELD

BULLET POINT

Story, Action, Result Template

STRENGTH

STORY

ACTION

RESULT

POSITION HELD

BULLET POINT

Story, Action, Result Template

STRENGTH

STORY

ACTION

RESULT

POSITION HELD

BULLET POINT

Story, Action, Result Template

STRENGTH

STORY

ACTION

RESULT

POSITION HELD

BULLET POINT

Story, Action, Result Template

STRENGTH

STORY

ACTION

RESULT

POSITION HELD

BULLET POINT

Story, Action, Result Template

STRENGTH

STORY

ACTION

RESULT

POSITION HELD

BULLET POINT

Story, Action, Result Template

STRENGTH

STORY

ACTION

RESULT

POSITION HELD

BULLET POINT

Story, Action, Result Template

STRENGTH

STORY

ACTION

RESULT

POSITION HELD

BULLET POINT

Story, Action, Result Template

STRENGTH

STORY

ACTION

RESULT

POSITION HELD

BULLET POINT

Story, Action, Result Template

STRENGTH

STORY

ACTION

RESULT

POSITION HELD

BULLET POINT

Story, Action, Result Template

STRENGTH

STORY

ACTION

RESULT

POSITION HELD

BULLET POINT

Story, Action, Result Template

STRENGTH

STORY

ACTION

RESULT

POSITION HELD

BULLET POINT

Story, Action, Result Template

STRENGTH

STORY

ACTION

RESULT

POSITION HELD

BULLET POINT

Story, Action, Result Template

STRENGTH

STORY

ACTION

RESULT

POSITION HELD

BULLET POINT

Story, Action, Result Template

STRENGTH

STORY

ACTION

RESULT

POSITION HELD

BULLET POINT

Story, Action, Result Template

STRENGTH

STORY

ACTION

RESULT

POSITION HELD

BULLET POINT

www.ingramcontent.com/pod-product-compliance
Lightning Source LLC
Chambersburg PA
CBHW081550170526
45166CB00009B/2651